*The S........*

*...ore*
*u will '*

For the people of Bradford

THE SAYINGS OF THE GREAT RELIGIOUS LEADERS

Editor: Andrew Linzey

**The Sayings of Jesus**

Selected by Andrew Linzey
Director of the Centre for the Study of Theology in the
University of Essex

**The Sayings of Moses**

Selected by Dan Cohn-Sherbok
University Lecturer in Jewish Theology in the University of
Kent

**The Sayings of Muhammad**

Selected and Translated by Neal Robinson
Senior Lecturer in Religious Studies in the Cheltenham and
Gloucester College of Higher Education

**The Sayings of the Buddha**

Selected by Geoffrey Parrinder
Emeritus Professor of Comparative Study of Religions in
the University of London, King's College

*The Sayings of*

# MUHAMMAD

### selected and translated
### from the Arabic by

### NEAL ROBINSON

**DUCKWORTH**

First published in 1991 by
Gerald Duckworth & Co. Ltd.
The Old Piano Factory
43 Gloucester Crescent, London NW1 7DY

Introduction, translation and editorial arrangement
© 1991 by Neal Robinson

**British Library Cataloguing in Publication Data**
The Sayings of Muhammad.
1. Islam
I. Robinson, Neal
297.63

ISBN 0-7156-2365-6

It gives me pleasure to thank Dr Ahmad al-Banna, for
discussing the translation with me, and Dr John Hughes,
for suggesting numerous stylistic improvements. Needless
to say, I bear sole responsibility for any remaining errors or
solecisms.

### Abbreviations

*Q* = Qur'ān. The numbers indicate the sūra and āya in the standard
Egyptian edition.

*SB* = Bukhārī, *Sahīh* ed. Ahmad Muhammad Shākir (Beirut: 'Ālam
al-Kutub, n.d.) 9 parts bound in 3. The numbers indicate the part and
page.

*MM* = Tabrīzī, *Mishkat al-Masābih* ed. Muhammad Nāsir ad-Dīn
al-Albānī, 3rd edition (Beirut: al-Maktab al-Islāmī, 1405 H / 1985 CE) 3
volumes. The number indicates the hadīth.

Tabrīzī's sources: B = Bukhārī; M = Muslim; T = Tirmidhī; AD =
Abū Dā'ūd; IM = Ibn Māja; N = Nasā'ī; IH = Ibn Hanbal; BQ =
Baihaqī; DR = Dārimī.

¶ before a quotation indicates that the first words are not those of
the Prophet.

(w) = weak.

Isnāds are omitted, but the name of the Companion is given.

Photoset in North Wales by
Derek Doyle & Associates, Mold, Clwyd
Printed in Great Britain by
Redwood Press Limited, Melksham

# Contents

# Introduction

Muhammad's native city, Mecca, had two principal claims to fame: it was a cult centre for pagan Arabs who came on pilgrimage to the Kaaba; and it controlled the trade which passed up and down the Western fringe of Arabia. Like many of the city's inhabitants, Muhammad's father was a merchant belonging to the tribe of Quraish. Muhammad never knew his father, for he died, while returning from a business trip shortly before Muhammad's birth in 570 CE. When he was only six his mother also died and for the next two years the orphan was cared for by his grandfather, 'Abd-al-Muttalib. Then, when he died too, Muhammad moved in with his uncle. Although the uncle, Abū Tālib, had succeeded 'Abd-al-Muttalib as head of the the clan of Hāshim, he was not a wealthy man and could not afford to set Muhammad up in business. He did, however, teach him how to engage in commerce, by taking him with him on a visit to Syria. When he was twenty-five Muhammad visited Syria again, this time acting as an agent for a wealthy widow, Khadīja bint Khuwaylid. So impressed was she by his honesty, and by the success of the enterprise, that she proposed to him. Although she was fifteen years his senior and had been married twice before, he accepted.

Muhammad's marriage to Khadīja brought him a change of fortune, but what happened to him fifteen years later was to change the course of history. At the age of forty he began to have visions and became convinced that he was receiving visitations from the angel Gabriel. God had called him to be a prophet. A few years later, supported by Khadīja and a small group of friends, he began to preach in public. The early revelations spoke of God's goodness and power and warned of the impending judgment. They summoned the people to Islam – submission to the one true God identified as the Lord of the Kaaba – and urged them to abandon idolatry and greed, and to express their gratitude to God in prayer and charitable acts. The stern ethical monotheism of the revelations provoked fierce opposition from the rich Meccan merchants, and when the situation deteriorated Muhammad encouraged some of his followers to seek refuge from persecution by temporarily emigrating to Abyssinia. Muhammad himself was relatively safe while he could rely on the protection of his uncle, but when both Abū Tālib and Khadīja died he too had to seek refuge elsewhere.

In 622 Muhammad and his fellow Muslims emigrated to Yathrib, where many of the inhabitants had already pledged themselves to his cause. It is this emigration, or *hijra*, which marks the beginning of the Muslim era. In Yathrib (now known as Medina) the Emigrants were at first thought of as a clan, with Muhammad as their chief; the *Ansār* (or 'Helpers') – the name given to the indigenous Muslims – looked on him as their religious leader while still paying temporal allegiance to their own chiefs. It was not long, however, before Muhammad established a theocracy with himself as the head of state, although not without bitter opposition from the Jews who comprised about a third of the population. The revelations which he received in Medina regulated Islam's principal religious practices, laid the foundations of Muslim law, and exhorted the believers to engage in armed struggle against idolatry. During the last ten years of his life Muhammad led many successful military campaigns, capturing Mecca and gaining hegemony over the Arabian Peninsula. He contracted a number of marriages, some of them with the widows of friends who had been killed in battle. In 632/11, when the Muslims were poised to overrun the empires of Persia and Byzantium, he died with his head on the lap of 'Ā'isha, his only virgin bride.

None of Muhammad's sons survived him – the youngest, Ibrāhīm, had died while still a small child only a few months earlier. The Shī'ites believe that the leadership of the Muslim community should have passed to 'Alī, who was the Prophet's cousin, the husband of his daughter Fātima and the father of Hasan and Hussein, his only grandchildren to reach adulthood. In fact 'Alī had to wait his turn, for he was three times passed over in favour of other Companions of the Prophet: Abū Bakr, 'Umar and 'Uthmān. 'Alī is revered by Sunnī Muslims as the fourth and last of the Rightly-guided Caliphs. After his assassination in 661/40 the Muslim empire, which now included Egypt, the Levant and Persia, was ruled by the Umayyads who moved the capital to the ancient city of Damascus. In 750/132 the Umayyads were ousted by the 'Abbasids who twelve years later founded Baghdad as their new capital.

During Muhammad's lifetime the revelations were committed to memory by his Companions and written down on palm leaves, scraps of papyrus or the bones of animals. After his death Abū Bakr gave orders for the material to be collected in book form and 'Uthmān subsequently promulgated the standard edition. It is widely accepted that, apart from a few orthographic improvements, the Qur'ān as we know it today is the same as that authorised by 'Uthmān. For Muslims this Book is not just Scripture, it is the uncreated Word of God. It should not be confused with the sayings of Muhammad. These are to be found in the collections of *hadīth* which were made at a much later date. The most authoritative collection is that of Bukhārī (d. 870/256). It comprises over 7,000 hadīth, although if we exclude variants and repetitions the figure is reduced to 2,762.

Each hadīth consists of two parts: an *isnād* and a *matn*. The isnād is a chain of guarantors beginning with the name of Bukhārī's informer and culminating in the name of one of the Companions of the Prophet. The matn is the subject matter of the hadīth and may be either a saying of Muhammad or a report about him. Bukhārī spent sixteen years compiling his collection, questioning over 1,000 sheikhs in Balkh, Merv, Nīshāpūr, Mesopotamia, the Hijāz, Egypt and Syria. He applied stringent tests to the isnāds and it is said that on one occasion, after travelling hundreds of miles to hear hadīth from a reputably pious man, he returned home without bothering to question him because he saw him deceiving his horse by attracting it with an empty nose-bag! There were many other collections besides Bukhārī's, but only five of them achieved canonical status: those made by Muslim b. Hajjāj, Abū Dā'ūd, Tirmidhī, Ibn Māja and Nasā'ī.

Opinions differ about the reliability of this vast corpus of hadīth. Many non-Muslim scholars express extreme scepticism. What is not disputed is the enormous amount of spurious material that was in circulation at the time when the six collections were made. Where some forgers had political or sectarian motives, others simply wished to promote practices which they cherished, or to honour the Prophet by attributing wise sayings to him. Unhappily others acted solely out of malice, like the man who confessed to having created 4,000 hadīth forbidding what is allowed or allowing what is forbidden. Then there were the story-tellers who made a living by pandering to the masses; one day, for instance, the traditionist al-A'mash entered a mosque in Basra and heard a story-teller narrating a spurious hadīth and putting his name at the beginning of the isnād! On hearing this, al-A'mash sat in the middle of the circle and started plucking hairs from his armpit. The story-teller rebuked him, but he replied: 'I am doing better than you... I am following the practice of the Prophet while you are telling lies. I am A'mash and I reported nothing of the sort.'

However, most Muslims hold that, despite the vastness of the task, Bukhārī and Muslim b. Hajjāj successfully separated the wheat from the chaff and only retained hadīth which were 'sound'. The other four compilers relaxed the criteria for admissibility and their collections contain numerous hadīth which they classified as 'good' or in some cases 'weak'. 'Good' hadīth are less authoritative than 'sound' ones but are generally held to be good enough for establishing points of law, whereas 'weak' hadīth may only be used for exhortation.

Whether or not the hadīth take us back to the Muhammad of history, they tell us a great deal about the Muhammad who lives in the Muslim imagination. They owe their authority to the Qur'anic injunction to obey God and His Messenger (*Q* 8.2 etc) and to the Qur'ān's assertion that the Messenger of God is a good example for believers (*Q* 33.21). For this reason Muslims regard him as the model of human perfection to be emulated in all aspects.

When compiling the present work I tried to preserve the structure of Bukhārī's collection in broad outline, though I have condensed the 97 main headings of that collection into 24. I supplemented my initial selection from Bukhārī by the addition of sayings from the *Mishkat al-Masābih* of Tabrīzī, which contains hadīth drawn from all six canonical collections and from others which are less authoritative. In carrying out the translation I aimed at good idiomatic English without sacrificing scholarly accuracy.

# The Revelation

The Qur'ān states that Gabriel brought the message down
to Muhammad's heart with God's permission (*Q* 2.97) and
mentions two occasions on which Muhammad's reception
of revelation was accompanied by a vision (*Q* 53.1-18, cf.
81.21-5).

*

¶ According to 'Ā'isha, the Mother of the Believers, when
al-Hārith b. Hishām said to the Prophet, 'Messenger of
God, how does the Revelation come to you?', he answered,
'At certain moments, it comes to me like the continuous
ringing of a bell, which is the worst for me. Then it stops
and I merely retain what the angel has transmitted to me.
On other occasions the angel presents himself to me in the
form of a man. He speaks to me and I understand what he
says to me.' 'Ā'isha added, 'Even on very cold days, I saw
the Prophet's forehead running with sweat the moment the
revelation stopped.'     *SB* 1.2

¶ 'Ā'isha, the Mother of the Believers, said, 'The Revelation
began for the Prophet as pious visions which he used to
have during his sleep. All these visions were as clear as
daylight to him. As a result he began to love spiritual
retreats. He withdrew to the cave of Hirā where he devoted
himself to *tahannuth* – acts of praise during a number of
consecutive nights without returning home. He used to
take provisions with him for this purpose. Then he would
return to Khadīja and take the provisions necessary for a
further similar retreat. That continued until the truth was at
last brought to him in this cave of Hirā. Then the angel
came and found him and said, "Read!" – "I can't read," he
answered. "The angel immediately grabbed me," narrated
the Prophet, "and squeezed me until I lost all my strength
and repeated the word 'Read!' – 'I can't read,' I answered
again. For the third time the angel grabbed me and
squeezed me until he had taken away all my strength.
Then he released me saying, 'Read, in the name of your

Lord who created. He created Man from a blood clot. Read, and your Lord is most generous' " [Q 96.1-3]

In possession of this message, the Prophet returned to Khadīja bint Khuwaylid, his heart pounding, and exclaimed, "Wrap me up! Wrap me up!" He was kept wrapped up until he had recovered from his fright. Then, addressing Khadīja, he explained what had happened, adding, "I feared for my life!" – "Never!" replied Khadīja, "God would never cause you affliction, for you look after your relatives, you support the weak, you give to the destitute, you are hospitable and you help those who have gone wrong to do right."

Then Khadīja led Muhammad to Waraqa b. Nawfal b. Asad b. 'Abd-al-'Uzza. This man, who was Khadīja's cousin on her mother's side, had embraced Christianity in pre-Islamic times. He knew how to write Hebrew characters and had copied in Hebrew part of the Gospel which God wished him to transcribe. At that time he was an old man and had lost his sight. "My cousin," Khadīja said to him, "listen to what the son of your brother has to tell you." – "Nephew," replied Waraqa, "what is it about?" The Prophet told him what he had seen. Waraqa said, "This is the Nāmūs whom God sent to Moses. Would that I were young now. Ah! How I could wish to be alive still when your fellow citizens banish you!" – "Will they drive me out?" exclaimed the Prophet. – "Yes," replied Waraqa. "No man has ever brought what you have brought without being opposed. If I am still alive on that day I will help you with all my strength." Soon after that Waraqa died and there were no more revelations for a time.'     *SB* 1.3

# Islām and Belief

The words *islām* (Islām or submission) and *imān* (faith or belief) are often used interchangeably. Strictly speaking, *imān* is something which has entered the heart whereas *islām* is more a matter of practice (cf. *Q* 49.14). The Qur'ān defines the content of belief as God, the last day, the angels, the Scripture and the prophets (*Q* 2.177).

\*

Islam is built on five pillars: the profession that there is no god but God and that Muhammad is the messenger of God; performance of the ritual prayer; payment of the obligatory charity; the pilgrimage; and the fast of Ramadān. *SB* 1.9, Ibn 'Umar

The true Muslim is one whose tongue and hand other Muslims do not fear. The true emigrant is one who flees what God has forbidden. *SB* 1.9, 'Abdallah b. 'Amr

When a man calls his fellow Muslim an infidel one of them certainly deserves that title! *SB* 8.32, Abū Hurayra

None of you really believes until he desires for his fellow Muslim what he desires for himself. *SB* 1.10, Anas

None of you is a complete believer unless he has more affection for me than he has for his father, for his children and for all the rest of the human race.
*SB* 1.10, Abū Hurayra

There are three things which, when you possess them, make you taste the sweetness of faith. First, to love God and his messenger more than all other beings. Secondly, to love others solely for God's sake. Finally, to detest the thought of lapsing into unbelief as much as the thought of being thrown into Hell. *SB* 1.10, Anas

Those who have merited Paradise will enter it, whereas the reprobates will enter Hell. Then God will say, 'Bring out from Hell those in whose heart there is faith, albeit no heavier than a grain of mustard seed.' So they will be brought out despite having been burnt to a cinder. Then they will be thrown into the river of life, and will sprout up just as seeds sprout by the side of a torrent. Haven't you seen them open out their tangled mass of yellow flowers?

*SB* 1.12, Abū Sa'īd al-Khudrī

For a Muslim, almost the best possible asset is sheep which he can lead to graze on the peaks of the mountains and in places watered by rain, thereby fleeing from temptation and taking his religion with him.

*SB* 1.11, Abū Sa'īd al-Khudrī

Three things are characteristic of a hypocrite: when he speaks he lies, when he makes a promise he fails to keep it, and when you put your trust in him he betrays it.

*SB* 1.15, Abū Hurayra

The value of an action depends on the intention. Everyone will be rewarded in accordance with the goal which he set himself. If he emigrated for the sake of God and His messenger, his emigration will be counted to him for God and His messenger. If he emigrated in order to gain something in this world, or to find himself a wife, his emigration will be counted to him for the goal which he set himself.

*SB* 7.4, 'Umar b. al-Khattāb

Every new-born child is by nature a Muslim. It is his parents who make a Jew, a Christian or a Zoroastrian of him. Likewise every animal is born whole; have you ever seen one born with its ears clipped?

*SB* 2.118, Abū Hurayra

Believer is to fellow believer as parts of a building which support each other. *SB* 8.14, Abū Mūsa

Modesty is an aspect of belief. *SB* 8.35, 'Abdallah b. 'Umar

¶ Ibn 'Umar said, 'The Prophet said, "The believer is like a green tree which never loses its leaves or bark." Some of the faithful said it was this tree, some that. I wanted to say that it was the palm tree but, as I was a young man, I was too modest to speak. Then the Prophet said, "It is the palm tree." ' *SB* 8.36

# Knowledge

In the Qur'ān, wisdom is described as a great gift (Q 2.269) and Muhammad is exhorted to pray for an increase in knowledge (Q 20.114).

*

Make it easy, not difficult. Proclaim good news and don't terrify your audience.                    SB 1.27, Anas

There are only two types of person you should envy: the man to whom God has given wealth and the power to spend it all in the cause of truth, and the man to whom God has given wisdom and who judges by it and teaches it.
                                           SB 1.28, 'Abdallah b. Mas'ūd

To Satan a single jurist is a more formidable opponent than a thousand ordinary worshippers.
                                           MM 217, T & IM, Ibn 'Abbās

Three people will have a double reward. First there is the Jew or Christian who believes in his own prophet and in Muhammad. Then there is the slave who fulfils his duty to God and to his masters. Finally there is the man who has a female slave whom he brings up well and instructs well before setting her free and marrying her; he too will have a double reward.          SB 1.35, the father of Abū Burda

For a wise man, a wise saying is like something he has lost. No matter where he finds it, he has the greater right to it.
                                           MM 216, T, Abū Hurayra

The person who goes in search of knowledge is on active service for God until he returns.     MM 220, T & DR, Anas

It is the duty of every Muslim male and female to seek knowledge. To impart learning to those who are unworthy of it is like decking out swine in necklaces of jewels, pearls and gold.                              MM 218, IM, Anas (w)

Learn the compulsory religious duties and the Qur'ān, and teach them to the people for I am mortal.

*MM* 244, T, Abū Hurayra

If, for the sake of my community, anyone commits to memory forty hadīth concerning the affairs of their religion, God will resurrect him as a jurist and I shall be an intercessor and a witness for him on the Day of Resurrection. *MM* 258, BQ, Abū Dardā'a

¶ Ibn 'Umar said, 'I heard the Messenger of God say, "While I was asleep I dreamed that I was brought a bowl of milk. I drank so much that I felt that the liquid was going to run out from under my nails. Then I gave 'Umar b. al-Khattāb what I couldn't drink." – "What interpretation do you give to that?" asked someone. "The milk was knowledge", he replied.' *SB* 1.31

Don't tell lies about me! Whoever tells lies about me will most certainly go to Hell. *SB* 1.38, 'Alī

At the beginning of every century God the Mighty and Majestic will raise up for this people someone who will renew their religion for them.

*MM* 247, AD, Abū Hurayra (w)

If you knew what I knew, you would laugh little and weep much. *SB* 8.127, Anas & Abū Hurayra

I know more about God than all of you and I am the most godfearing. *SB* 1.12, 'Ā'isha

Among the signs preceding the final Hour, knowledge will diminish and there will be manifest ignorance; adultery will be much in evidence; and men will diminish in number, whereas women will become so numerous that there will be no more than one man to support fifty women. *SB* 1.31, Anas

# Ritual Purity and Hygiene

The Qur'ān stresses the importance of purity of heart and mind (Q 26.89 & 91.9) as well as physical cleanliness (Q 74.4). It gives instructions concerning the ablutions to be performed before the ritual prayer (Q 5.6). These ablutions should be repeated after sleep or any bodily emissions.

*

When my people are summoned on the Day of Resurrection they will have bright marks on their foreheads, the traces of their ablutions. Any of you who can increase the size of these bright marks should do so! [cf. Q 75.24]. SB 1.46, Abū Hurayra

If it hadn't been too demanding for my people, I would have ordered them to clean their teeth before every prayer. SB 2.5, Abū Hurayra

Every time Gabriel came, he ordered me to clean my teeth – so much so that I was frightened I would wear them out! MM 386, IH, Abū Umāma

¶ Whenever the Prophet entered a lavatory he used to say: 'O God, I seek refuge with you from evil spirits both male and female.' SB 1.48, Anas

When you drink from a vessel don't breathe into it. When you go to the lavatory don't touch your penis with your right hand and don't use your right hand for wiping yourself. SB 1.50, Abū Qatāda

¶ Abū Ayyūb al-Ansārī said that the Prophet said, 'Don't defecate or urinate facing in the direction of prayer or with your back to it. Face eastwards or westwards instead.' Abū Ayyūb added, 'When we reached Syria we found that the lavatories had been constructed facing Mecca so we turned our heads to one side and asked God for forgiveness.' SB 1.109

If you start to doze off during the ritual prayer go away and sleep until you are in a fit state to know what you are reciting. *SB* 1.64, Anas

If you break wind during the ritual prayer, hold your nose and walk out. *MM* 1007, AD, 'Ā'isha

'Umar, don't urinate standing up. *MM* 363, T & IM, 'Umar

You certainly shouldn't urinate in stagnant water and then wash in it. *SB* 1.69, Abū Hurayra

¶ The Prophet said to me, 'Bring me the prayer mat from the mosque.' I said, 'I am having my periods.' He replied, 'You are not having them in your hands!' *MM* 549, M, 'Ā'isha

¶ 'Ā'isha said: 'The Prophet said, "When your periods arrive, stop performing the ritual prayer. Then, when they are finished, wash away the blood and pray." ' *SB* 1.90

Have a bath on Friday before attending the congregational prayers. *SB* 2.1, 'Abdallah b. 'Umar

The Children of Israel used to bathe completely naked and in full view of each other, whereas Moses bathed by himself. 'Good heavens!' they said, 'There can be only one thing stopping Moses bathing with us. He must have a scrotal hernia!' Now one day, when Moses went to bathe, he left his clothes on a rock. The rock ran off with them and Moses gave chase saying, 'My clothes, rock!' When the Children of Israel saw Moses they said, 'Good heavens! There's nothing wrong with him!' Moses retrieved his clothes and gave the rock a good beating. *SB* 1.78, Abū Hurayra

# Prayer and the Mosque

The Qur'ān refers to prayers at different times of the day (Q 2.238, 11.114, 17.78, 20.130, 50.39) and mentions bowing and prostrating (Q 2.125) in the direction of Mecca (Q 2.144). It also mentions the Friday prayer (Q 62.9f). The hadīth specify when the prayers should be performed, what words should be said and what actions should accompany them.

*

¶ Abū Hurayra said that the Messenger of God said, 'If one of you had a river right by his door and he bathed in it five times a day, do you think that there would be any dirt left on him?' They said, 'No, not a trace.' He said, 'That is how it is with the five prayers; by means of them God wipes away all sins.'                                          MM 565, B & M

Perfume and women have been made dear to me and for my sheer delight I have been given the ritual prayer.
                                          MM 5261, N & IH, Anas

Except for graveyards and bath-houses the whole earth is a mosque.                MM 737, AD, T & DR, Abū Saʿīd

During the call to prayer, Satan turns his back and farts so as not to hear it. When the first call is completed, he turns round again until the second call and then he turns his back once more. When it too is completed, he again turns round and tries to trouble the conscience of the believer by saying to him, 'Remember this, remember that', putting into the believer's mind things which he was not thinking about. In this way he endeavours to bring him to the point where he no longer knows where he has got to in his prayer.                                SB 1.158, Abū Hurayra

Every time you pray, God's face is turned towards you. So don't blow your nose in front of God during the prayer.
                                          SB 8.23, 'Abdallah b. 'Umar

When a person sleeps, Satan ties three knots in his nape. As he makes each knot he says, 'May the night be long for you! Sleep on!' When that person wakes up and mentions God, one of the knots is undone. When he performs the ablutions, another knot falls away and if he prays the final knot is loosed. Then in the morning he feels energetic and has peace of mind. Otherwise in the morning he will be troubled and sluggish. *SB* 2.65, Abū Hurayra

¶ Abū Hurayra said, 'We were talking in front of the Prophet about a man who had slept right through until morning without getting up to pray. The Prophet said, "Satan pissed in his ear." ' *SB* 2.66, 'Abdallah

Each night, when the night is two thirds spent, our blessed and exalted Lord descends to the nether heaven and says, 'If anyone invokes me, I will answer his prayer. If anyone asks me for something I will grant him it. If anyone seeks forgiveness I will forgive him'. *SB* 2.66, Abū Hurayra

To miss the afternoon prayer is as serious as losing your family and possessions. *SB* 1.145, 'Abdallah b. 'Umar

When you enter a mosque say, 'O God, open the doors of your mercy for me'; and when you leave say, 'O God, pray give me of your bounty.' *MM* 703, M, Abū Usayd

Prayer performed in company is twenty-seven times better than prayer performed alone. *SB* 1.166, 'Abdallah b. 'Umar

When three Muslims are together one of them must lead the prayer. The fittest person to do this is the most well-versed in the Qur'ān. *MM* 1118, M, Abū Sa'īd

Those who lead the prayer act on your behalf. If their prayers are correct, they will benefit you. If their prayers are defective it is they and not you who will be held responsible, and the prayers will still benefit you. *SB* 1.178, Abū Hurayra

Listen and follow the person leading the prayer even if he is an Abyssinian with a head like a raisin. *SB* 1.178, Anas b. Mālik

When I stand up to lead the prayer, I have a mind to pray slowly. But if I hear a child crying, I speed up the prayer for fear of causing distress to the mother. *SB* 1.181, Qatāda

When a woman asks you for permission to go to the mosque do not refuse her. *SB* 1.220, Abū 'Abdallah

When Friday comes round, the angels stand by the gate of the mosque writing down people's names on their arrival. The first person gains as much credit as if he had donated a fat she-camel to charity; the second as if he had given a cow; the third a ram; the fourth a chicken; and the fifth an egg. When the imām steps forward the angels fold their registers and listen to the sermon. *SB* 2.14, Abū Hurayra

O God, make it rain round about us not on us!
*SB* 2.40, Anas b. Mālik

There are five 'keys of the Unseen' known to none but God [cf. *Q* 6.59]. Nobody knows what will happen tomorrow. Nobody knows what will happen in the womb. No soul knows what his deeds will earn him tomorrow. No soul knows in what land he will die. Finally, nobody knows when the rain will come. *SB* 2.41, 'Abdallah b. 'Umar

The sun and the moon are not eclipsed for anyone's birth, nor for anyone's death. Solar and lunar eclipses are two of God's signs, so when you see them you should pray.
*SB* 2.48, Abū Mas'ūd

# Death and the Hereafter

The Qur'ān teaches that death takes place at the divinely appointed time (*Q* 16.61 & 69.42) and that the soul of the deceased is received by angels (*Q* 7.37 & 32.11). On the Day of Resurrection, the dead will be raised from their tombs and will be judged according to the works which they have sent ahead of them (*Q* 75.6-15, 82.4f, 84.4-7 etc). Some will be rewarded with Paradise (*Q* 43.68-73, 56.10-26 etc) but others will be punished in Hell (*Q* 38.55-8, 43.74-8 etc). Muhammad's mortality is explicitly mentioned (*Q* 3.144 & 15.99)

\*

A Muslim has five duties towards another Muslim: to return his greeting, to visit him when he is sick, to follow his funeral procession, to accept his invitation, and to pray for his health when he sneezes.     *SB* 2.90, Abū Hurayra

Never insult the dead. They are where their deeds had to lead them.     *SB* 8.134, 'Ā'isha

Three things follow a dead person to the grave and two of them return while one remains with him. His family, his wealth and his deeds follow him; his family return home with his wealth, but his deeds remain.

*MM* 5167, B & M, Anas

When a person dies the angels say, 'What has he sent in advance?' But human beings say, 'What has he left behind?'
*MM* 5219, BQ, Abū Hurayra

Even if there were a valley full of gold, Man would want two of them. Nothing but the dust of the grave will stop his mouth. Yet God will turn to those who repent.
*SB* 8.115, Anas b. Mālik

Jābir b. 'Abdallah said, 'When my father was killed, I was full of tears and wanted to uncover his face. The believers tried to stop me but the Prophet did not forbid me from doing it. Then, when my maternal aunt Fātima began to cry too, he said to her, "Whether you cry or not the angels will shelter him with their wings until you lay him to rest in the earth." '     *SB* 2.91

If any Muslim has had three of his children die in infancy, God will make him enter Paradise because of His extreme compassion for him.     *SB* 2.92, Anas

¶ Al-Barā' said, 'When Ibrāhīm died the Messenger of God said, "He will certainly find a wet-nurse in Paradise." '
SB 2.125, 'Adiyy b. Thābit

Our eyes are full of tears and our hearts are grief-stricken but we will not say anything that will displease our Lord. O Ibrāhīm, we are grief-stricken at being separated from you.
SB 2.105, Anas b. Mālik

¶ One day the Prophet passed by a woman who was weeping at a tomb. 'Fear God,' he said, 'and resign yourself.' She replied, 'Leave me alone! You have never been struck with such misfortune as I have.' The woman was informed that the person whom she had been speaking to was the Prophet. She went straight away to the Prophet's door and, not finding a door-keeper, she went inside and said, 'I didn't realise who you were.' He merely replied, 'True resignation consists uniquely in bearing the initial shock.'
SB 2.100, Anas b. Mālik

The deceased will be punished in his tomb for the groans uttered over him.
SB 2.102, 'Umar

O God, I seek refuge with you from the punishment of the tomb and the punishment of Hell, from the trials of life, of death and of the Antichrist.
SB 2.124, Abū Hurayra

When a dead person has been lowered into his tomb and his friends have gone away so that he can no longer hear their footsteps, he sees two angels come to him who make him sit up. They ask him concerning Muhammad, 'What do you say about this man?' If the dead person is a true believer he will say, 'I testify that he is God's servant and messenger.' Then the angels will say to him, 'Look at the place which you would have occupied in Hell. In exchange God has assigned you a place in Paradise.' Then the man will see both places at the same time. As for the hypocrite or the evil-doer, when he is asked the same question he will answer, 'I'm none too sure. I used to repeat what everyone else said.' Then the angels will say to him, 'So you knew nothing and you read nothing?' And they will beat him so violently with an iron rod that he will utter a cry which all the angels will hear although it will be inaudible to men and jinn.
SB 2.123, Anas b. Mālik

When you die, every morning and evening until the Day of
Resurrection you will be shown the place which you will
occupy in Hell or in Paradise with the words 'There's your
place!'                                   *SB* 8.134, Ibn 'Umar

A person who hangs himself will continue to hang himself
in Hell. A person who stabs himself will continue to do so
in Hell.                                  *SB* 2.121, Abū Hurayra

In Paradise there is a tree whose shade a horesman on a
swift and healthy steed could not cross in a hundred years.
                                  *SB* 8.143, Abū Saʿīd al-Khudrī

Whoever enters Paradise will be in bliss and not in want.
His clothing will not wear out and his youth will never
fade.                                  *MM* 5621, M, Abū Hurayra

By God! What is this world compared with the Hereafter! It
is like dipping your finger in the sea; look how little
remains on it when you withdraw it!
                                  *MM* 5156, M, Mustarid b. Shaddād

Be in this world as a stranger or as one who is passing
through.                              *SB* 8.110, ʿAbdallah b. ʿUmar

¶ ʿĀʾisha said, 'While he was well, the Prophet used to say
that no prophet had ever died before seeing the place
which he would occupy in Paradise and being given the
choice between this world and the next. When the illness
had weakened him he passed out with his head resting on
my thigh. Then he regained consciousness and, fixing his
gaze on the ceiling of the room, said, "O God, the more
exalted companion" [cf. *Q* 4.69]. Then I understood that he
had not chosen us and I remembered what he had said
while he was still well. Thus the last words which he spoke
were "O God, the more exalted companion".'

                                                      *SB* 6.18

# Zakāt, Charity and Gifts

The Qur'ān teaches that the poor and needy have a right to a share of other people's wealth (Q 51.19) and it warns of the dire consequences of hoarding one's goods (Q 3.180). Compulsory charity, or *zakāt* (literally 'that which purifies'), is an annual levy of about 2½ per cent of a person's disposable income which purifies him and sanctifies the remainder. Payment of *zakāt* is an expression of worship and is therefore frequently mentioned together with the performance of *salāt*, the ritual prayer (e.g. Q 2.43). The Qur'ān also encourages voluntary almsgiving and specifies those who are entitled to receive charity (Q 9.60).

*

Camels in better condition than they were on earth will advance on their owner who failed to pay *zakāt* on them and will trample him under foot, and sheep will butt him with their horns. You should milk your animals when they have drunk and give some of the milk as charity. On the Day of Resurrection none of you need come to me with a bleating sheep round his neck and plead 'Muhammad, intercede for me', for I shall tell him, 'I can't do anything for you. I told you before what you should do.' Nor need anyone come with a grumbling camel round his neck and make the same plea, for I shall simply reply, 'I can't influence God in your favour. I told you before what you should do.'                    *SB* 2.132, Abū Hurayra

I wouldn't want to have a heap of gold the size of Mount Uhud, unless I could spend it all in God's cause, bar the last three dinars.                    *SB* 2.134, Abū Dharr

The higher hand is better than the lower hand. The higher hand is the one that gives; the lower hand is the one that receives.                    *SB* 2.140, 'Abdallah b. 'Umar

Give charity because a time will come when a man will go round with his charity and not find anyone willing to accept it. The person to whom he offers it will say, 'Ah! If you had come yesterday I would have accepted it, but today I don't need it any more.' *SB* 2.135, Hāritha b. Wahb

Every single day each person has two angels near him who have descended from heaven. The one says, 'O God, compensate the person who gives charity.' The other says, 'O God, inflict a loss on the person who withholds his money.' *SB* 2.142, Abū Hurayra

Spend generously and do not keep an account; God will keep an account for you. Put nothing to one side; God will put to one side for you. *SB* 3.207, Asmā'

Avoid Hell by giving charity, even if it means sharing your last date, and, if you have nothing at all, by speaking a kind word. *SB* 8.144, 'Adiyy b. Hātim

The charitable person and the miser are like two men clothed in chain-mail from the breast to the shoulders. Every time the charitable man gives charity this tunic stretches over his skin with the result that it soon covers the tips of his fingers and protects his whole body. For the miser, on the other hand, when he wants to give charity each of the rings of this chain-mail becomes rusted in place, and when he tries to stretch it it won't stretch.

*SB* 2.142, Abū Hurayra

God will have no sympathy for the person who showed no sympathy for men. *SB* 9.141 Jarīr b. 'Abdallah

An old man's heart does not stop being young in two respects: in its love of the good things of this world and of fond hopes. *SB* 8.111, Abū Hurayra

Wealth does not consist in the abundance of possessions. Wealth is wealth of the soul. *SB* 8.118, Abū Hurayra

Muslim women, don't disdain to give a present to your neighbour even if you can only afford a sheep's trotter.
*SB* 3.201, Abū Hurayra

¶ 'Ā'isha said, 'Messenger of God, I have two neighbours. Which one ought I to give a present to?' He replied, 'The one whose door is nearest to you.' *SB* 3.208

A person who goes back on a gift he has made is like a dog which returns to its vomit. *SB* 3.207, Ibn 'Abbās

Ah! How fine a thing is the loan of a she-camel with its udders swollen with pure milk, or of a ewe which yields a bowlful of pure milk in the morning and another in the evening! *SB* 3.216, Abū Hurayra

Each joint of a believer's body should give charity. Every day that the sun rises, anyone who establishes justice among people performs a charitable act.

*SB* 3.245, Abū Hurayra

¶ A man came and found the Messenger of God and said to him, 'I'm done for!' – 'How come?' asked the Prophet. 'I had sex with my wife during the daytime in Ramadān,' he answered. 'Do you have a slave you can set free?' said the Prophet. 'No.' – 'Can you feed sixty poor people?' – 'No.' – While this was going on a man came in with a basket full of dates. 'Take this basket,' the Prophet said to the first man, 'and give it in charity.' – 'To someone more needy than me? I swear by Him who sent you with the Truth that there is not a house in Medina whose inhabitants are more needy than us.' – 'Take the basket,' said the Prophet, 'and feed your family with it.' *SB* 3.210, Abū Hurayra

The really poor person is not the one whom you send away after giving him a date or two, or one or two mouthfuls of food. The really poor person is the one who does not dare ask [cf. *Q* 2.273]. *SB* 6.40, Abū Hurayra

# Hajj; Mecca and Medina

The Qur'ān states that the Kaaba at Mecca was founded by Abraham (*Q* 2.125ff), and it stipulates that Muslims should go there on pilgrimage (*hajj*) and visit it at other times (*Q*

2.158,196-203, 5.94-6, 22.27-36 etc). It says relatively little about Medina (Q 9.101,120, 33.60, 63.8). The hadīth designate the pilgrimage as one of the five pillars of Islam and specify that it should be performed by every Muslim at least once in his life, provided that this does not cause hardship to his family. They describe in minute detail the clothing and deportment of the pilgrim and the prayers and rituals which he must perform. They also praise the merits of Medina.

\*

¶ 'Ā'isha, the mother of the believers, said, 'Messenger of God, we consider jihād the most excellent deed. So couldn't we engage in jihād?' – 'No,' he answered, 'but the most excellent jihād is the pilgrimage which has been performed devoutly.'                    *SB* 2.164

Anyone who performs the pilgrimage in order to please God, and while accomplishing it, does not have sex with his wife or behave immorally, will return home as he was on the day of his birth.                    *SB* 2.164, Abū Hurayra

After Gog and Magog have appeared, don't fail to perform the pilgrimage or to visit Mecca.
                    *SB* 2.182, Abū Saʿīd al-Khudrī

The person who destroys the Kaaba will be Old Thin Legs, an Abyssinian.                    *SB* 2.184, Abū Hurayra

I have received the order to go to a city which will devour the other cities. Some people call it Yathrib, but its name is Medina, the city which expels dishonest folk from its bosom as the bellows of the smithy drives out impurities from iron.                    *SB* 3.26, Abū Hurayra

Faith will take refuge in Medina as a snake takes refuge in its hole.                    *SB* 3.27, Abū Hurayra

The terror caused by the Antichrist will not penetrate Medina, for this city will then have seven gates with two angels stationed at each of them.        *SB* 3.28, Abū Bakr

O God, grant Medina double the blessings you have
bestowed on Mecca.                              *SB* 3.29, Anas

O God, make us have for Medina the affection we had for
Mecca, or even greater affection. O God, bless us in this
city, by causing our measures to be full. Make this city
healthy for us and transfer its fevers to Juhfa.
                                              *SB* 3.30, 'Ā'isha

Between my house and my pulpit there is one of the
gardens of Paradise.      *SB* 2.77, 'Abdallah b. Zayd al- Māzinī

# The Fast of Ramadān

Ramadān, the ninth month of the lunar calendar, is the
month in which the revelation of the Qur'an began.
Throughout this month, Muslims are required to abstain
from eating, drinking and sexual intercourse between
sunrise and sunset. All three activities are permitted at
night-time 'until the moment when you can distinguish the
white thread from the black thread' (*Q* 2.183-7). The actual
night on which Muhammad received his call is known as
the Night of Power. The Qur'an describes it as 'better than
a thousand months' (*Q* 97.3).

*

In Paradise there is a gate called al-Rayyān. Those who
have fasted will enter by it on the Day of Resurrection.
There will be an announcement asking, 'Where are those
who have fasted?' Then they will get up, and none but they
will enter by that gate. As soon as they have entered, the
gate will be closed and no one else will enter that way.
                                              *SB* 3.32, Sahl

When Ramadān arrives, Heaven's gates are opened, Hell's
gates are closed and the demons are chained up.
                                         *SB* 3.33, Abū Hurayra

The fast gives protection from Hell. The person who fasts should not have sex or behave foolishly. If someone picks a quarrel with him, he should simply say he is fasting and repeat it if necessary. I swear by Him who holds my life in His hands, that the stench of the mouth of a person who is fasting is a more agreeable to God than the smell of musk. God has said, 'To fast for Me is to give up eating, drinking and satisfying your passions. The fast is for My sake and I will recompense the person who fasts and repay all his good actions tenfold.'          *SB* 3.31, Abū Hurayra

As for the person who will not give up speaking and practising falsehood, God doesn't require him to give up his food and drink!          *SB* 3.33, Abū Hurayra

Do not begin the month of fasting until you have seen the crescent of the new moon, and do not terminate the month of fasting until you have seen the next new moon. If it is obscured by clouds when you think it should be visible, add an extra day.          *SB* 3.34, 'Abdallah b. 'Umar

We are an illiterate nation. We don't write and we don't perform calculations. The month varies in length – sometimes it has twenty-nine days, sometimes thirty.
          *SB* 3.35, Ibn 'Umar

¶ 'Adiyy b. Hātim said, 'When the verse "…until the moment when you can distinguish the white thread from the black thread…" was revealed, I went and took a black cord and a white cord and put them beneath my pillow. During the night I looked at them and was unable to distinguish between them. Early in the morning I went and found the Messenger of God and told him. He replied, "The two threads are the blackness of the night and the whiteness of the day." '          *SB* 3.36

Eat a light meal before daybreak during Ramadān. A blessing is attached to this meal.          *SB* 3.38, Anas b. Mālik

The person who inadvertently eats and drinks should continue the fast, because it is God who made him eat and drink.          *SB* 3.40, Abū Hurayra

When you break the fast, do so with dates. If you cannot find any dates, break the fast with water, because it is pure.
*MM* 1990, IH, T, AD, IM & DR, Salmān b. 'Amr

It is not an act of piety to fast while on a journey.
*SB* 3.44, Jābir b. 'Abdallah

Is it not the case that a woman stops praying and fasting during her periods? This is a lightening of her religious obligations. *SB* 3.45, Abū Sa'īd

The person who observes the fast of Ramadān with faith and attention will obtain the forgiveness of his past faults. The person who prays during the Night of Power with faith and attention will obtain the forgiveness of his past faults. *SB* 3.59, Abū Hurayra

Search for the Night of Power among the odd nights of the last ten nights of the month of Ramadān. *SB* 3.60, 'Ā'isha

¶ 'Ā'isha reported, 'I said, "Messenger of God, if I know which night is the Night of Power, what should I say during it?" He said, "Say, 'O God you are forgiving, and you love forgiveness, so forgive me.' " '
*MM* 2091, IH, IM & T

# Work, Commerce & Honesty

In the Qur'ān we are told that the daytime was created for man to earn his living (*Q* 78.11). Trade is permitted, but usury is forbidden (*Q* 2.275).

\*

Between what is clearly permitted and what is obviously illicit there are doubtful cases. The person who refrains from what he thinks might be sinful will be led to refrain from what is clearly illicit. The person who is inclined to do what he thinks might be sinful will be led to do what is obviously illicit. Sin is God's private pasture; if you graze in its vicinity, you will run the risk of entering it.

*SB* 3.69, an- Nu'mān b. Bashīr

Nobody ever eats a better meal than the one which he has earned with his own hands. God's prophet, David, used to eat what he gained by the work of his hands.

*SB* 3.74, al-Miqdām

Rather than beg off people who may or may not give you what you ask for, it is better to take some string and make bundles of firewood to sell so that God may preserve your dignity. *SB* 3.149, Az-Zubayr b. al-'Awwām

May God have mercy on the person who is generous when he buys, when he sells and when he asks to be repaid.

*SB* 3.75, Jābir b. 'Abdallah

There is as much difference between good company and bad as there is between a musk-seller and a blacksmith's bellows. No harm will come to you from the musk-seller; you will either buy some musk or enjoy its scent. But the blacksmith's bellows will burn your body or your clothes, and you will find the air from them foul-smelling.

*SB* 3.82, the father of Abū Mūsa

A rich person who defers payment commits an injustice.

*SB* 3.155, Abū Hurayra

Return even a needle and thread. Avoid embezzlement, because on the Day of Resurrection it will be a cause of shame for those who resorted to it.

*MM* 4023, DR, 'Ubāda b. as-Sāmat

# Jihād and Martyrdom

The root meaning of *jihād* is striving or expending effort, but the word is generally used in a technical sense to denote holy war against the infidels. The Qur'ān orders Muslims to expend effort for God's cause (*Q* 2.218 etc) and to fight for God's cause (*Q* 2.190 etc). It specifies that a fifth of the booty belongs to God and his Messenger, to be used for the common good (*Q* 8.41). It contains a promise that those killed in battle will have their sins forgiven and will be admitted to Paradise (*Q* 3.195).

*

Strive against the idolaters with your property, your lives and your tongues.          *MM* 3821, AD, N & DR, Anas

A single step on active service for God at the beginning or end of the day is preferable to this world and all that it contains.          *SB* 4.20, Sahl b. Sa'd

I have received orders to fight against people until they say that there is no god but God. The person who says this has nothing to fear from me as regards his person or his possessions, provided he fulfils his religious duties. It is God who will reckon with him.          *SB* 4.58, Abū Hurayra

The fire of Hell will not touch feet that are covered in dust gathered in active service for God.          *SB* 4.25, Abū 'Abs

March in the name of God, with God's aid and in accordance with the religion of the Messenger of God. Do not kill the old and feeble, young children or women. Do not defraud your leader, but collect your rightful share of the booty. Act well and show kindness, because God loves those who show kindness.          *MM* 3956, AD, Anas

O Men, do not yearn to encounter the enemy. Rather ask God to preserve you. Then, when you do encounter them, show endurance and know that Paradise is in the shadow of your sabres.          *SB* 4.62, Sālim Abū an-Nadr

Chosroes will perish and there will be no Chosroes after him. Caesar will certainly perish too and there will be no Caesar after him. Their treasures will be shared out in God's cause. *SB* 4.77, Abū Hurayra

¶ Abū Mūsa al-Ash'arī said, 'Once we were with the Prophet and had climbed the side of a valley. We raised our voices to shout "God is very Great" and "All praise to God". The Prophet said to us, "Restrain yourselves! The One whom you invoke is neither deaf nor absent; he is with you. He is all-hearing and close. Blessed be His name and exalted His majesty!" ' *SB* 4.69, Abū Mūsa al-Ash'arī

This religion will never cease to exist. A party of Muslims will always fight for it until the Hour comes to pass. *MM* 3801, M, Jabīr b. Samura

During the night I had a vision of two men who came to me and ascended with me to the tree which marks the confines of Paradise. Then they took me into a house which was finer and more magnificent than any I had never seen. They said to me, 'This house is the dwelling of the martyrs.' *SB* 4.20, Samura

Nobody who enters Paradise will want to return to this world, no matter what earthly goods he possessed. The sole exception is the martyr. He will yearn to return to this world to be killed again ten times over, knowing what he does of the honours awaiting him. *SB* 4.26, Anas b. Mālik

Whoever meets God without bearing any trace of having engaged in jihād, meets God with a defect in him. *MM* 3835, T & IM, Abū Hurayra

On the Day of Resurrection, the wounds received by Muslims in holy war will have the precise form they had when they were inflicted, and blood will gush from them again. It will be the colour of blood, but it it will smell like musk. *SB* 1.68, Abū Hurayra

Anyone who helps a widow or a pauper will gain as much merit as a person who engages in holy war or who prays at night and fasts by day. *SB* 7.80, Abū Hurayra

# The Prophets

The Qur'ān refers to Muhammad as the seal of the prophets (Q 33.40), and it mentions many of his predecessors. It includes extensive material about Abraham, Moses and Jesus, but the details often differ from those in the Jewish and Christian Scriptures, which Muslims generally hold to have been corrupted (cf. Q 2.75, 4.46 etc). Jesus is described as a word and spirit from God (Q 4.171), but he is only God's human servant (Q 43.59) and messenger (Q 5.75), not His son (Q 9.30). He prophesied the coming of Muhammad (Q 61.6), and his own return is perhaps alluded to (Q 43.61). According to tradition Muhammad met many of the prophets on the night when he was taken from Mecca to Jerusalem and thence to heaven (cf. Q 17.1)

*

During the night two visitors came and found me and led me to a man who was so tall that I could hardly see his head. It was Abraham.                                    SB 4.170, Samura

On the Day of Resurrection, Abraham will meet his father Azar, whose face will be covered with grime and dust, and will say to him, 'Didn't I tell you not to disobey me?' [cf. Q 6.75, 19.41-8] The father will reply, 'I won't disobey you now.' Then Abraham will say, 'My Lord, you promised not to put me to shame when the dead are raised. What greater shame could there be for me than to see my father estranged from God?' God Most High will reply, 'I have decreed that Paradise is forbidden to infidels.' Then someone will say, 'Abraham, what's that at your feet?' And Abraham will see a hyena all spotted with blood. The animal will be seized by the paws and thrown into Hell.
                                    SB 4.169, Abū Hurayra

On the Day of Resurrection everyone will be struck unconscious. I shall be the first person to come round and then I shall see Moses clinging to one of the feet of God's throne. I don't know whether he will have come round before me or whether he will have been spared because he was struck unconscious on Sinai [cf. Q 7.143].

*SB* 4.187, Abū Saʻīd

While Job was naked and washing himself, a swarm of golden locusts landed on him. So he began to gather them up in his clothes. Then his Lord called to him, 'Eh! Job, haven't I made you rich enough without those things.' – 'Certainly Lord,' he replied, 'but I shall never be rich enough to do without your blessing' [cf. Q 21.83].

*SB* 4.184, Abū Hurayra

An impish jinn pounced on me last night in order to interrupt me in my prayer. When God had helped me get the better of him, I wanted to tie him to one of the pillars of the mosque so that you could all see him when morning came. But I remembered the words of my fellow prophet Solomon, 'My Lord forgive me and bestow on me a power the like of which none after me will have' [Q 38.35].

*SB* 4.197, Abū Hurayra

Solomon son of David said, 'Tonight I am going to visit seventy women and each will conceive and give birth to a horseman who will fight for God's cause.' You should say, 'God willing,'* remarked his companion. Since Solomon didn't add those words, only one of the women became pregnant and she gave birth to a child with half its body missing. If Solomon had said 'God willing' they would all have borne him sons who would have fought for God's cause. [*in shāʾ allah: cf. Q 2.70 etc.]   *SB* 4.197, Abū Hurayra

If anyone testifies that there is no god but the One God who has no associates; that Muhammad is His servant and His messenger; that Jesus is God's servant and messenger, His word addressed to Mary and a spirit from God; that Paradise really exists and that Hell really exists, God will cause him to enter Paradise regardless of his actions.

*SB* 4.201, ʻUbāda

Hardly a single descendant of Adam is born without Satan touching him at the moment of his birth. A baby who is touched like that gives a cry. The only exceptions are Mary and her son [cf. Q 3.36].   *SB* 4.199, Abū Hurayra

Among men I am the closest to Jesus Son of Mary in this world and the next. The prophets are brothers; although they have different mothers, their religion is one.

*SB* 4.203, Abū Hurayra

While I slept, I had a vision in which I saw myself circumambulating the Kaaba. Then I noticed a brown-skinned man with smooth hair which was wet; water was dripping from it onto the ground between his legs. I asked who it was and was told, 'It is the Son of Mary.' As I continued, I noticed another man. He was red-faced, very fat and had frizzy hair. Moreover he was blind in the right eye and his good eye revolved in its orbit like a grape. I asked who it was and was told, 'The Antichrist.' The man who most resembles him is Ibn Qatan.

*SB* 4.203, Abū Sālim

I swear by Him who holds my life between His hands, the son of Mary will come back down among you very soon as a just judge. He will break crosses, kill pigs and abolish the tax which Jews and Christians pay in return for their religious freedom. Wealth will be so abundant that nobody will accept it. When this happens, one prostration will be better for you than this world and all that it contains.

*SB* 4.205, Abū Hurayra

Do not extol me as the Christians have extolled the Son of Mary. I am only God's servant. Refer to me as the servant and messenger of God.          *SB* 4.204, 'Umar

Jābir b. 'Abdallah said, 'We were gathering arak fruits with the Messenger of God and he told us, "Choose the blackest. They're the best." When he was asked whether he had ever guarded sheep he replied, "There is not a single prophet who has not guarded them." '          *SB* 4.191

Don't believe what the Jews and Christians tell you, but don't call them liars either. Say, 'We believe in God and in what has been revealed to us …' [Q 2.130]

*SB* 6.25, Abū Hurayra

The vision of a believer is the forty-sixth part of the gift of prophecy.          *SB* 9.39, 'Ubāda b. Sāmit

The person who sees me in a dream really sees me because
Satan never takes on my appearance.

*SB* 9.43, Abū Saʿīd al-Khudrī

# The Merits of the Companions

Most of the persons mentioned in this section were
referred to in the Introduction. Abū Dharr was a notorious
robber who surprised the Prophet by his early conversion
to Islam. Saʿd b. Muʿādh was a Medinan clan chief who
became a leading member of the Ansār. For sayings about
Khadīja and ʿĀʾisha see the section on Women, Marriage
and Divorce.

*

The best people of my community are my contemporaries
and supporters; then those of the next generation; then
those of the generation after that.  *SB* 5.2, ʿImrān b. Husayn

¶ Anas b. Mālik said, 'The Prophet, accompanied by Abū
Bakr, ʿUmar and ʿUthmān, went up Mount Uhud and it
began to tremble beneath them. Tapping the earth with his
foot, the Prophet said, "Stand firm, Uhud, for you only
have a prophet, a sincere friend and two martyrs standing
on you." '                                        *SB* 5.14

¶ Anas reported that Abū Bakr said, 'When I was with the
Prophet in the cave, I said to him, "If one of them were to
think of looking beneath his feet he would see us." He
replied, "Abū Bakr, what do you think could happen to two
people who have God with them as the third?" '  *SB* 5.4

If I had to choose a bosom friend from my people it is Abū
Bakr whom I would choose. Yet why choose him as a
bosom friend, when in Islam he is my brother and
companion!                                *SB* 5.5, Ibn ʿAbbās

In my sleep I had a vision of myself drawing water from a well with a bucket attached to a pulley. Then Abū Bakr came and drew one or two buckets with some difficulty; God will forgive him! Next 'Umar b. al-Khattāb arrived and the bucket was transformed into a large one. I have never seen a chief of his people do such wonderful things! So everyone was able to quench his thirst and rest.

*SB* 5.13, 'Abdallah b. 'Umar

'Uthmān, God may dress you in a shirt. If they want to divest you of it don't take it off for them.

*MM* 6068, T & IM, 'Ā'isha

¶ According to Sa'd b. a. Waqqās the Prophet said to 'Ali, 'Are you not pleased that your position in relation to me is that of Aaron in relation to Moses?' *SB* 5.24

'Alī is special to me and I am special to him; he is the supporting friend of every believer.

*MM* 6081, T, 'Imrān b. Husayn

Fātima is part of me; whoever upsets her upsets me.

*SB* 5.26, al-Miswār b. Makhrama

Hasan and Hussein are my two joys in this world.

*MM* 6155, Ibn 'Umar

The sky has not cast shade, nor the earth raised up green plants growing luxuriantly, for anyone who more resembles Jesus son of Mary in truthfulness and trustworthiness than Abū Dharr. *MM* 6230, Abū Dharr

God's throne shook at the death of Sa'd b. Mu'ādh.

*SB* 5.44, Jābir

# The Qur'ān

The Qur'ān itself stresses that the revelations were in Arabic (Q 12.2, 46.12 etc). We are also told that recitation of the Qur'ān at dawn is witnessed by angels (Q 17.78). There are many hadīth about Qur'anic interpretation and about the merits of the various sūras.

*

The worthiest of you is the one who learns the Qur'ān and then teaches it.                                    SB 6.236, 'Uthmān b. 'Affān

A believer who recites the Qur'ān is like a citron which smells good and tastes good. A believer who doesn't recite the Qur'ān is like a date which has no scent but tastes sweet. A hypocrite who recites the Qur'ān is like a myrtle berry which smells good but tastes bitter. A hypocrite who doesn't recite the Qur'ān is like a colocynth which has no scent and tastes bitter.                        SB 7.99, Abū Mūsa al-Ash'arī

Take great care with the Qur'ān, for I swear by Him who holds my life in His hands that it can slip away from you more easily than camels escape the cords with which they are hobbled.                                        SB 6.238, Abū Mūsa

A person in whose breast there is nothing of the Qur'ān is like a ruined house.             MM 2135, T & DR, Ibn 'Abbās

¶ Abū Hurayra reported that the Messenger of God said, 'Would you be pleased if you went home and found three big fat pregnant she-camels?' – 'Yes!' we replied. He said, 'Three verses of the Qur'an recited during prayer are better than three big fat pregnant she-camels.'             MM 2111, M

'Say: He is God, the One' [Q 112.1] is equivalent to a third of the Qur'ān.                          MM 2127, M, Abū ad-Darā'a

A person who has an excellent knowledge of the Qur'ān is with the noble pious scribes [cf. Q 80.15f]. A person who recites the Qur'an and keeps trying to pronounce the difficult passages where he gets tongue-tied, will have a double reward.              *MM* 2112, B & M, 'Ā'isha

If the Qur'ān were wrapped in a skin and then thrown into the fire it would not burn [i.e. a person who learns it by heart and acts on it will not burn in Hell].
                            *MM* 2140, DR, 'Uqba b 'Āmir

Ibn 'Umar reported that the Messenger of God said, 'These hearts become rusty just as iron becomes rusty when it comes into contact with water.' Someone said, 'Messenger of God, what is the remedy?' He replied, 'Frequent recollection of death and recitation of the Qur'ān.'
                            *MM* 2168, BQ, Ibn 'Umar (w)

Adorn the Qur'ān with your voices.
              *MM* 2199, IH, IM, AD & DR, Barā'a b. 'Āzib

Love the Arabs for three reasons: because I am an Arab, because the Qur'ān is in Arabic, and because Arabic is the language spoken in Paradise.      *MM* 5997, BQ, Ibn 'Abbās (w)

# Women, Marriage and Divorce

The Qur'ān states that devout men and women will be rewarded alike (Q 33.35). The only woman mentioned by name is Jesus' mother, Mary the daughter of 'Imrān (Q 3.35-47, 19.16-33 etc.) who, together with the wife of Pharaoh, is said to have been a model believer (Q 66.11f). Although women have similar rights to men they are slightly inferior to them (Q 2.228 & 4.34) and the testimony of two women is equivalent to that of one man (Q 2.282). A man may marry up to four women (Q 4.3), but the Prophet was given a special dispensation to marry more than this (Q 33.50) and his wives were known as 'Mothers of the

Believers' (*Q* 33.6). The mutual affection of husband and wife is stressed (*Q* 2.187 & 30.21). Provision is made for divorce (*Q* 2.227-41).

*

The best women ride camels. The devout women of the Quraish are the kindest with young children. They are also the best at looking after their husbands' possessions.
*SB* 7.7, Abū Hurayra

There have been many perfect men but the only perfect women were Mary the daughter of 'Imrān and Asiya the wife of Pharaoh. The superiority of 'Ā'isha over other women is like that of *tharīd** over other dishes. [*a dish of sopped bread, meat and broth.]
*SB* 5.36, Abū Mūsa al-Ash'arī

The best woman in her time was Mary the daughter of 'Imrān and the best woman in her time was Khadīja.
*SB* 4.200, 'Alī

¶ According to 'Ā'isha the Messenger of God said, 'I saw you in a dream. The angel led you to me and you were covered in a piece of silk material. "Here is your wife," he said. I removed the garment from your face and there you were. So I said, "If this is from God, He will bring it to pass." '
*SB* 7.19

Umm Salama, don't cause me trouble on account of 'Ā'isha. By God, there is not a woman among you under whose bed-covers I have received revelation, apart from her!
*SB* 5.37, Abū Hishām

Isn't the testimony of a woman worth only half the testimony of a man? That is because of her inferior intelligence.                    *SB* 3.326, Abū Sa'īd al-Khudrī

A man should never be alone with a woman unless she is chaperoned by a woman whom she is forbidden by law from marrying.                    *SB* 7.48, Ibn 'Abbās

Take care of women because woman was created from a rib. Now the most crooked part of a rib is the upper part. If you try to straighten it you will break it and if you leave it alone it will always remain crooked. So take care of women.                                   *SB* 4.161, Abū Hurayra

For every human being, God has foreordained an element of adultery which that person will inevitably commit: the glance which is the adultery of the eyes, and the word which is the adultery of the tongue. Men will always be subject to carnal desires, whether or not they gratify them.
                                                           *SB* 8.156, Abū Hurayra

Young people, if you are capable of supporting a family you should marry. If you are not, then fast, because fasting will protect you.                          *SB* 7.3, 'Abdallah b. Qays

A man marries a woman for four qualities: her wealth, her good family, her beauty, and her piety. Win the one who is devout. Otherwise perish your fortune!
                                                             *SB* 7.9, Abū Hurayra

The whole of this world is an object of delight and the best object of delight in this world is a devout woman.
                                                 *MM* 3083, M, 'Abdallah b. 'Amr

Beware of suspicion for a suspicion is more deceitful than a remark. Don't snoop. Don't probe. Don't hate one another. Be brothers. None of you should ask the hand of a woman whose hand has been asked already by his brother. Instead he should wait until his brother marries her or stops asking for her.                                        *SB* 7.24, Abū Hurayra

A grown-up girl is to be asked whether she consents to marriage. If she is silent it counts as assent. If she refuses she is not to be compelled.
                                         *MM* 3133, T, AD & N, Abū Hurayra

If someone, whose religion and character please you, seeks to marry your daughter, give your permission. For if you don't, there will be dissension in the land and widespread immorality.                           *MM* 3090, T, Abū Hurayra

For two people who love each other, you will find nothing to compare with marriage.          *MM* 3093, IM, Ibn 'Abbās

When a worshipper of God has taken a wife he has perfected half of his religion. So let him fear God in the other half.                    *MM* 3096, BQ, Anas

Women can be as alluring as Satan and will egg you on like Satan. If you fancy a woman and become infatuated with her, go and make love to your wife. It will help you get her out of your system!                    *MM* 3105, M, Jābir

How can you beat your wife like a bull-camel when a moment later you will make love to her!
                    *SB* 8.18, 'Abdallah b. Zam'a

When a husband invites his wife to sleep with him and she refuses, the angels curse her until the morning.
                    *SB* 7.39, Abū Hurayra

If, when you have intercourse with your wife, you say, 'O my God, keep Satan far from us, and far from that which you bestow on us', and a child is born from this union, Satan will not be able to harm the child.
                    *SB* 1.48, Ibn 'Abbās

¶ A man said, 'Messenger of God, we have sex with our female captives and we don't want them to lose their value. What do you think of *coitus interruptus*?' – 'Do you do that?' said the Prophet. 'Ah well! There's no harm in it, because every single life which God has decided to bring into existence will come into existence.'
                    *SB* 3.109, Abū Sa'īd al-Khudrī

¶ Sa'd b. Waqqās reported that a man came to the Prophet and said, 'I am avoiding sex with my wife.' The Messenger of God asked him, 'Why are you doing that?' The man replied, 'I am frightened of harming the child in her womb.' The Messenger of God said, 'If it were harmful, it would have harmed the Persians and Byzantines.'     *MM* 3188 M

Whoever has a son born to him should give him a good name and educate him. Then, when he reaches maturity, he should get him married. For when a son reaches maturity and his father doesn't get him married, if the son sins the father will be held responsible.
                    *MM* 3138, BQ, Abū Sa'īd & Ibn 'Abbās

In the Torah it is written, 'If a man's daughter reaches twelve years of age and he does not give her in marriage, then if she commits sin that sin will fall upon him.'

*MM* 3139, BQ, 'Umar b. al-Khaṭṭāb & Anas b. Mālik

A journey is a piece of torture, for it deprives you of sleep and food. So, when you have finished your business, hurry back to your wife and family.   *SB* 7.100, Abū Hurayra

When you return home after a long absence, don't knock on the door late at night.   *SB* 7.50, Jābir b. 'Abdallah

I was shown Paradise and I saw that most of its inhabitants were poor people. I was shown Hell and I saw that most of its inhabitants were women.   *SB* 8.118, 'Imrān b. Husayn

¶ One day the Prophet said, 'I was shown Hell and I noticed that it was above all populated with women who had been ungrateful.' When asked whether they had been ungrateful to God he replied, 'No, they were ungrateful to their husbands. They didn't recognise the benefits they had received. If you showered one of them with kindness all your life and she then found an occasion to reproach you for something she would say, "You've never been good to me." '   *SB* 1.14, Ibn 'Abbās

Of all lawful things, the one which God dislikes most is divorce.   *MM* 3280, AD, Ibn 'Umar

# Food and Etiquette at Meals

The Qur'an permits most foods, including fish (*Q* 5.96) and game caught by hunting dogs (*Q* 5.5). It forbids only carrion, blood, pork and all animals which have been

beaten to death or strangled or which have been
slaughtered in the name of any but God (*Q* 5.3). Wine is
forbidden on earth (*Q* 5.90) but it will abound in Paradise
(*Q* 47.15).

*

Feed the hungry, visit the sick and set captives free.
*SB* 7.87, Abū Mūsa al-Ashʿarī

If you are invited to a marriage feast, go.
*SB* 7.31, ʿAbdallah b. ʿUmar

If anyone invites me to dine on a shoulder of mutton, or
merely a sheep's trotter, I will accept.
*SB* 3.201, Abū Hurayra

I don't eat reclining.                    *SB* 7.93, Abu Juhayfa

Food which has not had God's name remembered over it,
Satan regards as easy prey.         *MM* 4160, M, Hudhayfa

When a man enters his house and remembers God on
entering and at meal-time, Satan says to his minions, 'No
shelter for you tonight and no dinner either.' When he
enters it without remembering God, Satan says, 'Shelter for
the night!' Then, if he doesn't remember God at meal-time
either, Satan says, 'Shelter for the night and dinner as well!'
*MM* 4161, M, Jābir

¶ Abū Wāqid al-Laythī reported that when the Prophet
arrived in Medina he found that the inhabitants had a
liking for camel humps and that they used to cut the fat
tails off sheep. He said, 'Anything which has been cut off a
live animal is carrion. It is not to be eaten.'
*MM* 4095, T & AD

Lizards I don't eat, but others may.      *SB* 7.125, Ibn ʿUmar

¶ Salman reported that the Prophet was asked about
locusts. He said, 'I don't eat most of the hosts of God, but
you are not forbidden to eat them.'          *MM* 4134, AD

Eat olive oil and anoint yourselves with it, because it comes from a blessed tree [cf. *Q* 24.35].

*MM* 4221, T, IM & DR, Abū Usayd al-Ansārī

People who have eaten garlic should keep clear of our mosques! *SB* 7.105, Anas

Those who drink wine in this world, and do not change their ways, will be forbidden it in the future life.

*SB* 7.135, Ibn 'Umar

They call the vine generous, yet nothing is generous apart from the believer's heart. *SB* 8.52, Abū Hurayra

I was made to ascend as far as the Lotus and there I saw four rivers – two of which are visible and two concealed. The two visible ones were the Nile and the Euphrates; the two concealed were rivers of Paradise. I was brought three goblets: one of milk, one of honey, and one of wine. I chose the goblet of milk and drank it. Then I was told, 'You have chosen the right way for yourself and your people.'

*SB* 7.141, Anas b. Mālik

¶ 'Umar b. a. Salama said, 'When I was a boy I was brought up by the Messenger of God. Since I used to put my hand in the dish on all sides, the Messenger of God said to me, "Now my boy, invoke the name of God, eat with your right hand, and eat what is in front of you." From that day I have always eaten as he told me.' *SB* 7.88

Don't eat or drink with your left hand, for Satan eats with his left hand and drinks with it. *MM* 4163, M, Ibn 'Amr

¶ Ibn 'Abbas reported that a large bowl of *tharīd* was brought to the Prophet. He said, 'Eat from the sides of it. Don't eat from the middle, because the blessing descends in the middle.' *MM* 4211, T & IM

¶ Anas b. Mālik reported that the Messenger of God was brought milk mixed with water, while a bedouin was sitting on his right and Abū Bakr was on his left. He drank some of it and then gave it to the bedouin with the words, 'To the right, to the right.' *SB* 7.144

Don't cut your meat with a knife. That is what foreigners do. Tear it off with your teeth for it is pleasanter and tastier.
                                        *MM* 4215, AD, 'Ā'isha

If a fly falls in your dish plunge it in completely before fishing it out, because in one of its wings there is disease and in the other there is the antidote.
                                        *SB* 7.181, Abū Hurayra

A meal for two is enough for three, a meal for three is enough for four.                 *SB* 7.92, Abū Huraya

A believer has only one gut, an infidel has seven.
                                        *SB* 7.93, Abū Hurayra

Don't belch so much, for on the Day of Resurrection the hungriest person will be the one who most often had a full stomach in this world.           *MM* 5193, T, Ibn 'Umar

My Lord offered to make the valley of Mecca full of gold for me. I said, 'No, My Lord. I prefer to be well-fed one day and hungry the next, so that when I am hungry I am humble towards you, and remember you and when I am well-fed I praise you and give you thanks.'
                                    *MM* 5190, IH & T, Abū Umāma

If your servant brings you a meal, and you don't make him sit with you, at least give him one or two mouthfuls or morsels, for he has had to bear the heat and trouble involved in preparing your food.    *SB* 7.106, Abū Hurayra

When dinner has been served, and the time of prayer arrives, eat first.               *SB* 7.107, Anas b. Mālik

When you have finished eating, don't wipe your hand until you have licked it.              *SB* 7.106, Ibn 'Abbās

¶ Abū Sa'īd al-Khudrī reported that when the Prophet finished his meal he used to say, 'All praise to Him who has given us food and drink and made us Muslims.'
                                    *MM* 4204, T, AD & IM

# Animals

According to the Qur'ān, all animals and birds belong to communities (Q 6.38) and give praise to God (Q 24.41). Hence the Prophet ordered his followers to be merciful even when slaughtering animals for food or killing dangerous species.

*

Kindness to any living creature will be rewarded.
*SB* 8.11, Abū Hurayra

¶ 'Abdallah b. 'Amr reported that the Messenger of God said, 'Whoever kills a sparrow or anything larger than a sparrow, without treating it as it has a right to be treated, will be answerable to God for killing it.' Someone said, 'Messenger of God, how does it have a right to be treated?' He said, 'To be slaughtered and eaten, not to to have its head cut off and be thrown away.'     *MM* 4094, IH, N & DR

God has prescribed that all things should be done well. If you kill, kill well. If you slaughter, slaughter well. Sharpen your blade and spare the suffering of the animal you slaughter.     *MM* 4073, M, Shaddād b. Aws

Don't shorten the forelocks of horses or their manes or their tails. For their tails keep off the flies, their manes keep them warm, and blessings are knotted in their forelocks.
*MM* 3880, AD 'Ubta b. 'Abd-as-Sulamī (w)

When you hear a cock crow, ask God's favour – for the cock has seen an angel. When you hear a donkey bray, seek God's protection from the accursed Satan – for the donkey has seen Satan.     *MM* 2419, B & M, Abū Hurayra

Do not abuse the cock. It rouses people for prayer.
*MM* 4136, AD, Zayd b. Khālid

Men are like camels: there is hardly one in a hundred that you would trust with your life.  *SB* 8.130, 'Abdallah b. 'Umar

A believer is not bitten twice by an animal which comes out of the same hole. *SB* 8.38, Abū Hurayra

When one of the prophets was bitten by an ant, he had the ant-hill burned. Then God revealed to him, 'Because of a single ant which bit you, you have burned an entire community who praised God!' *SB* 4.75, Abū Hurayra

When a snake appears in a dwelling place say to it, 'We ask you by the covenant of Noah and by the covenant of Solomon son of David, not to harm us.' If it returns, kill it. *MM* 4137, T & AD, Abū Laila

If you kill a wall gecko at a single blow, a hundred merits will be credited to your account. To kill it with two blows is less meritorious. To kill it with three is less meritorious still. *MM* 4121, M, Abū Hurayra

A woman went to Hell for tying up a she-cat without giving her anything to eat, or letting her feed herself on wild animals. *SB* 4.157, Ibn 'Umar

Whoever keeps a dog – unless it is a sheep-dog, a hunting dog, or one which guards the crops – has his merits daily diminished by a carat. *MM* 4099, B & M, Abū Hurayra

# Sickness and Medicine

Sickness and other calamities are described in the Qur'ān as trials by which God tests the sincerity of the believer (e.g. *Q* 29.2f). Honey and the Qur'ān itself are said to have healing power (*Q* 16.68f & 41.44).

*

There are two divine favours which many people fail to acknowledge: health and leisure.

*SB* 8.109, Ibn 'Abbās

No calamity ever befalls a Muslim without God erasing some of his faults on that occasion – even if the calamity is a minor one like being pricked by a thorn.

*SB* 7.148, 'Ā'isha

Yes indeed! No Muslim ever experiences suffering without God removing his sins, which fall away like leaves from a tree.                           *SB* 7.149, 'Abdallah b. Mas'ūd

When God has a person's well-being in mind, He inflicts him with trials.                       *SB* 7.149, Abū Hurayra

When a Muslim is sick or on a journey, the good works which he is in the habit of doing when he is at home or in good health are credited to his account.

*SB* 4.70, Abū Burda

A believer is like the tender young stem of a plant: wind from any direction makes it bend, but when the wind ceases it straightens up as does the believer after an ordeal. A wicked person is like a rigid and proud cedar until the day when God breaks it, if He so wishes.

*SB* 7.149, Abū Hurayra

None of you should wish for death when afflicted by illness. If you cannot stop yourself, then say, 'O God make me live as long as life is better for me, but make me die if it is better for me that way.'        *SB* 7.156, Anas b. Mālik

Do not wish for death. For if you are a good person you could do more good deeds, and if you are an evil-doer you could repent and gain God's favour.

*SB* 9.104, Sa'd b. Ubayd

God has not sent any sickness down to earth without at the same time sending a cure for it.      *SB* 7.158, Abū Hurayra

Healing can be obtained by three things: a potion of honey, cupping, and cauterisation. I forbid my people to use cauterisation.                        *SB* 7.159, Ibn 'Abbās

'Urwa said that 'Ā'isha used to prescribe *talbīna** for the sick
and those who had recently suffered bereavement, and
that she used to say, 'I heard the Messenger of God say,
"Talbīna soothes a patient's heart-burn and helps overcome
grief." ' [*a mixture of milk, bran and honey.]   *SB* 7.161

Black onion seeds contain a remedy for everything except
death.                                  *SB* 7.160, Abū Hurayra

Use aloes-wood because it is the remedy for seven
illnesses. It should be sniffed for a sore throat, and put in
the corner of the mouth for pleurisy.
                              *SB* 7.161, Umm Qays bint Mihsan

Truffles are like manna. Their sap is a remedy for eye
complaints.                             *SB* 7.164, Sa'īd b. Zayd

¶ Abū Sa'īd said, 'A man came and found the Prophet and
said to him, "My brother's bowels are upset." – "Give him
some honey to drink," replied the Prophet. The man gave
his brother a potion of honey. When he came back he said,
"I made him drink some but it only made him worse." –
"God has spoken the truth," said the Prophet, "it is your
brother's bowels which lied." '            *SB* 7.166

¶ Abū Hurayra said, 'The Messenger of God said, "There is
no contagion from sickness, nor from cholera, nor is a
screech owl a bad omen." – "Messenger of God", retorted a
bedouin, "how is it that my camels, which are like gazelles
amongst the dunes, become mangy when a mangy camel
mixes with them?" – "Who infected the first one?" replied
the Prophet.'                              *SB* 7.166

Do not go to a country where you know there is the plague.
However, if it breaks out in the country where you are,
don't leave in order to flee from it.
                              *SB* 7.169, 'Abd-ar-Rahmān b. 'Awf

Fever comes from the blaze of Hell. Put it out with water.
                                        *SB* 7.167, Ibn 'Umar

To be struck down by an intestinal ailment or by the plague
is to die a martyr.                       *SB* 7.169, Abū Hurayra

Two cures are prescribed for you: honey and the Qur'ān.
*MM* 4571, IM & BQ, from 'Abdallah b. Mas'ūd

When you visit a sick person tell him to pray for you
because his prayer is like that of the angels.
*MM* 1588, IM, 'Umar b. al-Khattāb

For a Muslim to visit a fellow Muslim who is sick is to be in
a garden of Paradise until he returns.
*MM* 1527, M, Thawbān

Whenever a Muslim pays an early morning visit to another
Muslim who is sick, seven thousand angels pray for him
until evening. If he visits him late in the evening, seven
thousand angels pray for him until morning and there is a
garden for him in Paradise.          *MM* 1550, T & AD, 'Alī

# Clothes and Grooming

The Qur'ān states that clothing was given by God for
concealment (*Q* 7.26). Women are required to dress
modestly (*Q* 24.31).

*

God will not look at a person who drags his garment
behind him out of conceit.          *SB* 7.182, 'Abdallah b. 'Umar

The part of the robe which hangs below the ankles will
burn in Hell.                        *SB* 7.183, Abū Hurayra

How many women who are well-dressed in this world will
be naked on the Day of Resurrection!
*SB* 7.197, Umm Salama

The person who wears silk in this world will never wear it
in the next!                         *SB* 7.193, Anas b. Mālik

Don't drink from vessels of gold or silver. Don't wear garments of silk or brocade. They have those things in this world, whereas you will have them in the world to come.

*SB* 7.146, Hudhayfa

¶ Al-Barā'a said, 'The Prophet was given a silk garment as a gift and we started feeling it with our hands and admiring it. The Prophet said, "Do you admire this?" We said, "Yes." He said, "In Paradise, the handkerchiefs of Sa'd b. Mu'ādh will be better than this." '

*SB* 7.194

When you put your shoes on, begin with the right foot; when you take them off, begin with the left. The right foot should be the first to be shod and the last to be unshod.

*SB* 7.199, Abū Hurayra

Don't walk with only one shoe. Either go barefoot or wear shoes on both feet.

*SB* 7.199, Abū Hurayra

Observe these practices which men should find natural: circumcision, shaving off the pubic hair, trimming the moustache, cutting the nails, and removing the hair from under the armpits.

*SB* 7.206, Abū Hurayra

The Jews and Christians don't dye their hair, so do differently from them.

*SB* 7.207, Abū Hurayra

Do contrary to the idolaters: let your beards grow, but trim your moustaches.

*SB* 7.206, Ibn 'Umar

God curse any woman who wears false hair or tattoos, or encourages others to do so!

*SB* 7.212, Abū Hurayra

# Miscellaneous Advice

Most of the sayings brought together under this heading refer to vices or virtues mentioned in the Qur'ān. For instance the Qur'ān warns against usury (*Q* 2.275ff), devouring the wealth of orphans (Q 4.11), and defaming the character of women (Q 24.4-9). It stresses the importance of truthfulness (Q 9.120), of mastering anger (Q 3.128), and of being dutiful towards one's parents (Q 17.23f, 31.24), one's mother in particular (Q 56.15).

\*

¶ Abū Hurayra said, 'A man came and found the Messenger of God and said to him, "Messenger of God, who has the most right to be well treated by me?" He replied, "Your mother." So the man asked, "And then who?" He replied, "Your mother." The man asked, "And then who?" He replied, "Your mother." Again the man said, "And then who?" He replied, "And then your father." '

*SB* 8.2.

¶ Jāhima came to the Prophet and said, 'Messenger of God, I have come to consult you because I intend to take part in a military campaign.' The Prophet said, 'Do you have a mother?' – 'Yes,' replied Jāhima. He said, 'Stay with her; Paradise is at her feet.'

*MM* 4939, IH, N & BQ, Mu'āwiya b. Jāhima

When you see someone more favoured than you in fortune and good looks, think of the person who is less favoured than you in those respects. *SB* 8.128, Abū Hurayra

Truthfulness leads to piety and piety leads to Paradise. A person should always be truthful so as to merit the name Very-truthful. Lying leads to immorality and immorality leads to Hell. Man keeps on lying until he is marked down in God's eyes as an inveterate liar. *SB* 8.30, 'Abdallah

Avoid seven dangers: idolatry, magic, taking human life (except when it is lawful to do so and not forbidden by God), usury charging interest, devouring an orphan's property, fleeing on the day of battle, and slandering women believers who would not think of doing wrong.

*SB* 4.12, Abū Hurayra

¶ One day the Prophet heard a man praise another man in an exaggerated way. He said, 'Do you want to be the fellow's downfall and to destroy him?' *SB* 8.22, Abū Mūsa

The person who tries to reconcile others is not a liar because his good words are well-intentioned.

*SB* 3.240, Umm Kulthūm bint 'Uqba

If you really must praise someone, say, 'I think such and such about him', provided that it seems to be true. For God will call you to account and nobody will plead your case with Him. *SB* 8.22, Abū Bakra

¶ A man said to the Prophet, 'Give me some advice.' He replied, 'Don't lose your temper.' The man repeated his request several times and each time the Prophet answered, 'Don't lose your temper.' *SB* 8.35, Abū Hurayra

Strength is not a matter of winning a fight. It is a matter of controlling your temper. *SB* 8.34, Abū Hurayra

¶ I heard the Messenger of God say, 'When two Muslims meet each other sword in hand, the one who kills and the one who is killed will go to Hell.' I said, 'Messenger of God, that will be the fate of the killer, but what about the one who is killed?' He replied, 'He was eager to kill his companion.' *SB* 9.5, Abū Bakra

The person who kills a man to whom he is bound by an agreement will not smell the scent of Paradise although that scent can be smelled from the distance of a forty-year march. *SB* 9.16, 'Abdallah b. 'Amr

Gabriel kept on advising me to take care of my neighbour; so much so that I thought he wanted me to make him my heir. *SB* 8.12, 'Ā'isha

# Greetings

The Qur'ān stipulates that when a person is greeted he should return the greeting or give a better one (*Q* 4.86). The godfearing will be greeted with the words *as-salāmu 'alaykum* (Peace be upon you!) as they enter Paradise (*Q* 39.73). This is the usual Muslim greeting; the reply is *wa-'alaykum as-salām* (And upon you peace!).

\*

God created Adam sixty cubits tall. When He created him, He told him, 'Go and greet some of the angels sitting over there and listen to the formula they use in reply because it will be yours and that of your posterity.' Adam said to them, 'Peace be upon you.' They replied, 'And upon you peace and the blessing of God.' It was the angels who added the words 'and the blessing of God'. Whoever enters Paradise will do so in the form of Adam despite the fact that people have continued to diminish in stature.

*SB* 8.62, Abū Hurayra

¶ A man asked the Prophet, 'Which Islām\* is the best?' He said, 'Feed and greet with peace those whom you know and those whom you do not know'. [\*the word Islām comes from the same root as *salām* (peace).]

*SB* 8.65, 'Abdallah b. 'Amr

The person who gives the greeting first is free from vanity.

*MM* 4666, BQ, 'Abdallah b. Mas'ūd

The rider should greet the person on foot, the person who is walking should greet the person who is seated, the small group should greet the more numerous group.

*SB* 8.64, Abū Hurayra

The youngest should greet the eldest, the passer-by the person who is seated, and the small group the more numerous group.

*SB* 8.64, Abū Hurayra

¶ 'Ā'isha said, 'A group of Jews entered the presence of the Messenger of God saying, *as-sāmu 'alaykum* [i.e. Death be upon you! – scarcely distinguishable in Arabic from the Muslim greeting]. Understanding their intention, I replied, "Death and curses be on you!" – "Go easy, 'Ā'isha!" exclaimed the Messenger of God. "God likes us to be polite in all circumstances." – "But didn't you hear what they

said?" I replied. "Well," he retorted, "I said, 'And on you too!'" '
*SB* 8.70

When the Jews and Christians greet you, reply, *wa-'alaykum* – 'And on you too!'
*SB* 8.71, Anas b. Mālik

The person who imitates non-Muslim greetings is not one of us. Do not imitate the Jews and Christians, for the Jews greet each other by pointing with their fingers and the Christians by pointing with the palms of their hands.
*MM* 4649, T, the grandfather of 'Amr b. Shu'ayb (w)

# Poetry, Music & Art

The Qur'an mentions demon-possessed poets who led people astray (*Q* 26.221-6) and it criticises Muhammmad's opponents for supposing that he himself was a mere poet (*Q* 21.5, 36.69, 37.36, 52.29f & 69.40-2). Nevertheless, in the Medinan period three poets – Hassān b. Thābit, Ka'b b. Malik and 'Abdallah b. Rawāha – used their skills in the cause of Islām. Hence the Prophet's ambivalent attitude. Music is not mentioned in the Qur'an but the harsh statements of the Prophet cited below are to some extent mitigated by other hadīth which permit its use at weddings and festivals. The Prophet's opposition to images and pictures is in line with the Qur'anic abhorrence of idolatry.

*

There is wisdom in poetry.
*SB* 8.42, Ubayy b. Ka'b

¶ Al-Barā'a reported that the Prophet said to Hassān, 'Unleash your satires. Gabriel will be with you.' *SB* 8.45

The truest word uttered by a poet is the word of Labīd, 'Is not everything, besides God, vain.' *SB* 8.43, Abū Hurayra

Better a belly full of pus than a belly full of poetry.

*SB* 8.45, Ibn 'Umar

¶ Anas said that on the day of the Battle of the Ditch the Ansār said:
   It is we who our oath to Muhammad did give
   And vowed we'd fight well as long as we lived.
And the Prophet answered them:
   O My God the only life is the life to come
   Reward Ansār and Emigrant for what they've done.

*SB* 4.61

¶ Jundab said that while the Prophet was walking he tripped over a stone and when his finger began to bleed he said,
   It's only a finger covered with blood,
   Alas, not a wound gained fighting for God.     *SB* 8.43

Singing makes hypocrisy grow in the heart as water makes crops grow.     *MM* 4810, BQ, Jābir

¶ Anas reported that the Prophet had a camel-driver called Anjasha who had a fine voice. The Prophet said to him, 'Steady on Anjasha! Don't break the glasses*!' [*an allusion to the women, either because they would be shaken if the camels went too fast or because they might be seduced by the singing.]     *SB* 8.58

Angels will not enter a house in which there are dogs and pictures.     *SB* 7.215, Abū Talha

The people who produced these pictures will be punished on the Day of Resurrection and will be told, 'Give life to what you have created!'     *SB* 7.215, 'Ā'isha & Ibn 'Umar

¶ Anas said, ''Ā'isha had a cloth with pictures on it which she had used as a hanging in one of the corners of her apartment. The Prophet said to her, "Take that away from here because those pictures keep on distracting me while I am saying my prayers." '     *SB* 7.216

# Justice and Oppression

The Qur'ān calls on men to obey God, His messenger and those in the authority (*Q* 4.58). It condemns oppression (*Q* 14.42) and requires rulers to establish justice (*Q* 38.26) and to take counsel with their subjects (*Q* 3.158 & 42.38). It prescribes amputation as a punishment for theft (*Q* 5.38).

\*

Whoever obeys me, obeys God; whoever rebels against me, rebels against God. Whoever obeys my delegate, obeys me; whoever rebels against my delegate, rebels against me.
*SB* 9.77, Abū Hurayra

¶ When the Prophet sent Mu'ādh to Yemen he told him, 'Dread the plea uttered by the oppressed, for no veil separates it from God.' *SB* 3.169, Ibn 'Abbās

All of you are shepherds responsible for your flocks. A ruler is shepherd of his subjects and he is responsible for them. A man is shepherd of his family and he is responsible for them. A woman is shepherd of her husband's home and she is responsible for it. A servant is shepherd of his master's wealth and he is responsible for it.
*SB* 2.6, 'Abdallah b. 'Umar.

¶ The Messenger of God said, 'Help your fellow Muslim whether oppressor or oppressed.' Anas said to him, 'Messenger of God, we will help the oppressed, but how do you expect us to help the oppressor?' – 'By preventing him from doing evil!' he answered. *SB* 3.168

A person who is killed defending his property is a martyr.
*SB* 3.179, 'Abdallah b. 'Amr

If people were given everything they sued for they would sue for men's lives and property. But the oath is the prerogative of the defendant. *MM* 3758, M, Ibn 'Abbās

It is for the plaintiff to bring proof. The oath is the prerogative of the defendant.

*MM* 3769, T, the grandfather of Shu'ayb.

¶ Abū Umāma reported that the Prophet said, 'God will make Hell obligatory and Paradise unlawful for whoever defrauds a Muslim on oath.' A man asked, 'Even if it is a small thing, Messenger of God?' He said, 'Even if it is only a twig of arak!' *MM* 3760, M

On the Day of Resurrection God will take the earth in His fist, fold up the sky with His right hand and say, 'Where are the kings of the earth?' *SB* 9.142, Abū Hurayra

The name which will be most hated by God on the Day of Resurrection is the name of the man who styles himself King of Kings. *SB* 8.56, Abū Hurayra

In your greed, you eagerly seek positions of authority, but you will regret it on the Day of Resurrection. To breast-feed an infant is commendable; to be over-eager to wean one is despicable! *SB* 9.79, Abū Hurayra

¶ Miqdām b. Ma'dī Kirba reported that the Messenger of God tapped him on the shoulder and said, 'Miqdām, my dear fellow, you will certainly gain salvation if you die without becoming a ruler, a scribe or an administrator.' *MM* 3702, AD (w)

¶ Abū Bakr said, 'On the day of the Battle of the Camel, God favoured me by bringing to my knowledge the following words, "When the Prophet learned that the Persians had enthroned the daughter of Chosroes he exclaimed, 'No people will ever prosper if it confides its authority in a woman.' " ' *SB* 9.70

The Muslim is the brother of any other Muslim. He should not oppress him or surrender him. If a Muslim comes to the aid of his brother in Islām, God will come to his aid.

*SB* 9.28, 'Abdallah b. 'Umar

O people, what led your predecessors astray was that they let the noble person who had stolen go unpunished, whereas if the thief was a humble person they carried out the sentence. I swear by God that if Fātima the daughter of Muhammad stole, Muhammad would cut her hand off.

*SB* 8.199, 'Ā'isha

Compromise is lawful for Muslims except a compromise which makes a lawful thing unlawful or an unlawful thing lawful. Muslims should stand by their terms except a term which makes a lawful thing unlawful or an unlawful thing lawful. *MM* 2923, T, AD & IM, 'Amr b. 'Awf

¶ Abū Humayd al-Sā'idī said, 'The Prophet had charged a man of the Banū Asad, called Ibn al-Utabiyya, to collect voluntary charity. When this man returned, he said, "This belongs to you and this was given to me as a present." Then the Prophet mounted the pulpit, praised God and proclaimed His glory and said, "What can one say about this agent whom we sent and who came and said, 'This is yours and this is mine'? He ought rather to have stayed at home with his mother and father to see whether anyone brought him presents there! By Him who holds my life in His hands, I swear that this man will not carry off a single thing received in that manner without being forced to carry it round his neck on the Day of Resurrection, be it a snorting camel, a lowing cow or a bleating sheep!" Then the Prophet raised his arms so high that we saw the white of his armpits and he cried out three times, "Have I fulfilled my mission?" ' *SB* 9.88

The best jihād is to speak a true word to a tyrannical ruler.

*MM* 3705, T, AD & IM, Abū Sa'īd

There is no obedience in transgression. You should only obey when you are ordered to do what is good.

*MM* 3665, B & M, 'Alī

# The Unity of God

The unity of God is the central doctrine of the Qur'ān. Some of the traditions in this section are extra-Qur'anic revelations known as *hadīth qudsī*. Their substance was revealed to Muhammad but he was left to express them in his own words.

\*

God created clemency and on the day He created it He divided it into a hundred parts. He kept ninety-nine parts in reserve for His own use and endowed all the beings whom He had created with the hundredth part. If the infidel knew how much clemency God had kept in reserve, he would not despair of Paradise. If the believer knew how much punishment God had kept in reserve he would not feel safe from Hell.                    *SB* 8.123, Abū Hurayra

When it comes to putting up with insults there is no one more long-suffering than God. Folk allege that He has a son but despite that, He forgives them and provides for their needs.                    *SB* 9.141, Abū Mūsa al-Ash'arī

¶ The Messenger of God said, 'Before the creation God wrote these words, "My clemency has outstripped My wrath." They are written close to Him, above His throne.'
                    *SB* 9.196, Abū Hurayra

¶ According to Hudhayfa when the Prophet retired to his bed he used to say, 'O God, it is by Your will that I live and that I die.' When he woke up the next day he used to say, 'Praise be to God who has made us live after causing us to die. It is for Him that the final resurrection will take place.'
                    *SB* 9.146

¶ The Messenger of God said, 'God says, "I live up to My servant's expectations. I am with him every time that he mentions Me. If he mentions Me to himself, I mention him to Myself. If he mentions Me in company, I mention him in even better company. If he draws near to Me by a span, I draw near to him by a cubit. If he draws near to Me by a cubit, I draw near to him by a fathom and if he walks towards Me, I quicken My pace towards him." '

*SB* 9.148, Abū Hurayra

On the Day of Resurrection you will see the Lord as you see this full moon. You won't need to push each other to one side to see Him. *SB* 9.157, Jarīr

God has ninety-nine names, one less than a hundred. The person who knows them by heart will enter Paradise.

*SB* 9.145, Abū Hurayra

¶ The Messenger of God said, 'When God loves one of His servants He says to Gabriel, "God loves so and so. You must love him as well." So Gabriel loves that person. Then Gabriel calls to the inhabitants of heaven, "God loves so and so. You must love him as well." So the inhabitants of heaven love that person. Moreover, as a result of this he prospers on earth.' *SB* 4.135, Abū Hurayra

¶ The Messenger of God said, 'God Most High has said, "I shall be at war with anyone who shows hostility to a devoted servant of Mine. Nothing is more pleasing to Me as a means for My servant to draw near to Me than the religious duties which I have imposed on him. My servant continues to draw near to Me with additional voluntary acts of devotion so that I love him. When I love him I am the Hearing with which he hears, the Sight with which he sees, the Hand with which he strikes and the Feet with which he walks. Whenever he asks Me for anything I give it to him. Whenever he asks Me for refuge I grant him it." '

*SB* 8.131, Abū Hurayra